TALES FROM THE TOUCHLINE

JÜRGEN KLOPP

HARRY CONINX

RAVEN

To Daisy, for all your help from beginning to end

This is a fictionalised biography describing some
of the key moments (so far!) in the career of
Jürgen Klopp.
Some of the events described in this book are
based upon the author's imagination and are
probably not entirely accurate representations
of what actually happened.

Tales from the Touchline
Jürgen Klopp
by Harry Coninx

Published by Raven Books
An imprint of Ransom Publishing Ltd.
Unit 7, Brocklands Farm, West Meon, Hampshire GU32 1JN, UK
www.ransom.co.uk

ISBN   978 180047 243 3
First published in 2023

Rotherham Libraries	
B55 088 762 6	
PETERS	04-Apr-2023
J920KLO	6.99
CHILD	RTTHY

CONTENTS

I

THE BIGGEST TROPHY

June 2019, Wanda Metropolitano Stadium, Madrid, Spain
Champions League Final, Liverpool v Spurs

"We're into the last hour now. Last chance for changes."
Pep Lijnders leaned forward and looked at Jürgen Klopp,
careful to make sure he wasn't being overheard by the
squad.

Jürgen adjusted his glasses nervously.

"We'll stick with what we've got," he replied. "Same
as we've done all season."

The stage was set for the biggest game of Liverpool's 2018-19 season – the UEFA Champions League final.

Liverpool had fought hard to get here. They'd come second in their group, behind French Champions PSG. They'd knocked out German Champions Bayern Munich. Then they'd come from 3-0 down to beat Spanish Champions Barcelona in the semi-finals.

It had been an improbable run to the final.

"So, we're not changing, then," Lijnders remarked. "Same front three and same defence."

Over the last year, Liverpool had found great success with a vibrant, dynamic front three, comprising Sadio Mané, Roberto Firmino and Mohamed Salah. The trio had scored the bulk of Liverpool's goals, aided by rampaging full-backs Trent Alexander-Arnold and Andy Robertson.

Jürgen knew it would be risky to play his open, attacking style in a final. He knew that it often left Liverpool exposed in defence – he'd seen it in the 3-0 first-leg defeat to Barcelona in the semis.

"We don't change," Jürgen asserted. "This is the football we play. Whatever the occasion."

His assistant, Lijnders, nodded. He hadn't been expecting any changes – he knew his boss well enough.

"But enough about us," Jürgen continued.

"You thinking about Harry Kane?" Lijnders asked, reading Jürgen's mind.

Tottenham's star striker had suffered from injury for most of the season, and had been racing to get fit for the final. Nobody knew whether he'd be lining up for Tottenham, or if they'd go with the alternative, Lucas Moura.

"What's the verdict then?" Jürgen asked.

"He's in," Lijnders said, looking down at the team sheet.

"Eriksen, Alli, Son, Kane," Lijnders continued, reading out the names of Spurs' forwards.

"I'd have been more concerned if Moura was starting," Jürgen admitted. "Kane won't be at 100% – he won't drag our defenders around. We can handle him."

"Anything else?" Lijnders asked.

"Not yet. Let the lads settle – we don't want them over-thinking things. We want clear heads."

In fact, Jürgen was trying to clear his own head. This wasn't his first final – it wasn't even his first Champions League final.

He thought back to the 2013 final, when his Borussia Dortmund team had narrowly lost to Bayern Munich. He'd never expected to be back competing on Europe's biggest stage.

But he still hadn't won anything with Liverpool. In his first year in charge, they'd lost the Europa League and League Cup finals. Last season, they'd been beaten in the final of this same competition by Real Madrid.

Just two weeks ago, he'd missed out on the Premier League title by a single point – to Manchester City.

He'd built a team capable of sweeping the very best aside, but he was yet to get them over the line. He was yet to win a trophy.

He was determined to change that today.

Now, just five minutes before kick-off, it was time for him to talk to his players. He got to his feet, silencing the chatter in the room.

All eyes turned towards him.

"Last year, we lost," he said. "We were beaten by a

good team. We made mistakes and we were punished. Tonight, we play another good team."

He paused, sizing up his players, searching their faces for any signs that they weren't up for it.

"They have Kane, Eriksen, Alli and Son. These guys are dangerous. We can't be hesitant. But if we play like we have done all season, we will win."

He looked around the room, letting his words sink in.

"We've been here before – we know what it takes to win these games. Forget the occasion. Forget the final. Just go out there and play a game of football. Enjoy it. These are the moments that make your careers."

The time for talking was over. Moments later, Jürgen was sitting next to Pep Lijnders in the dugout as the game kicked off.

"An early goal would be nice," Lijnders remarked with a grin.

As if his wishes were granted, Liverpool were awarded a penalty in the opening minutes, after a handball from Moussa Sissoko.

Mohamed Salah, Liverpool's top scorer, dutifully stepped up and converted the spot-kick. 1-0.

"Already better than last year," Jürgen murmured.

The game quickly fell into a slow, frustrating rhythm, with both teams struggling to create chances.

At half-time it was still 1-0, but Jürgen was frustrated. This wasn't the Liverpool he had created. They were in control, but it wasn't exciting – it wasn't the brilliant attacking play he wanted.

"Keep it up, guys," Jürgen told them in the dressing room. He knew he had to choose his words carefully. After all, they were still winning – he didn't want to damage morale.

"A bit more intensity, we get that second goal, we put them under pressure – and we see this game out," he added.

Fifteen minutes into the second half, Jürgen turned to his bench.

Divock Origi had been the surprise hero in the semi-final against Barcelona, with a brace in a 4-0 win at Anfield. He was the man Jürgen turned to now.

"Divock!" he called. "Come here!"

He wrapped his arm around his striker.

"You've scored some important goals this year,"

Jürgen told him. "Time to grab another. Spurs will push up soon – there's going to be space."

He was right. Spurs began to push, throwing on an attacking player in Lucas Moura. Liverpool were the ones defending now. A big challenge from Virgil van Dijk, then a huge save from Alisson in goal.

Jürgen had strengthened his defence in the transfer market, making some wise choices – and now they were paying off.

With a few minutes left, it looked as if Liverpool were holding on for a 1-0 win.

Then a Liverpool corner was lifted into the box. It looped up in the air, falling at the feet of the substitute, Divock Origi.

He took one touch and blasted it into the bottom corner.

GOAL!

The Liverpool fans erupted as the Liverpool players swarmed Origi.

"The sub scoring again. How about that?" Henderson shouted above the noise. "The gaffer knows what he's doing!"

Liverpool had their second goal – the one that would win them the game and the Champions League.

Moments later, the game was over. Jürgen had won his first trophy with Liverpool.

Not just *a* trophy, but the biggest trophy in the world.

Now Jürgen's name would be remembered alongside legendary managers such as Guardiola, Ancelotti and Mourinho. He would stand beside Liverpool heroes like Paisley and Shankly.

He was at the peak of his career. He'd proved that his Liverpool side could compete with the very best – and beat them.

Now they had their eyes firmly fixed on the Premier League. *He* was going to be the man to win Liverpool their first Premier League title. He was going to cement himself in their history books.

2
STEEP SLOPE TO SUCCESS

December 1980, Glatten, Germany

"Jürgen! Are you coming?" Jürgen's dad, Norbert, shouted to him as he marched through the snow. His two older sisters, Isolde and Stefanie, were also ahead of him and making good progress up the hill.

"I'm coming!" Jürgen grunted.

He flung his skis over his shoulder and trudged through the thick snow until he was alongside his father.

"You wanted to come out here, Jürgen," Norbert chuckled, clapping him on the back.

"It's fun," Jürgen panted, flashing him a smile that came out as more of a grimace, as he felt the pain in his legs.

Norbert, Isolde and Stefanie were keen athletes who enjoyed a wide range of sports. Jürgen wanted to prove that he belonged out on the slopes with them, even if he was still only 13.

"It's OK if you don't like it," Norbert smiled. "Some people only really get into one sport."

"No, I like all of them," Jürgen replied.

He wanted to be like his father, but until now Jürgen had been focusing on just the one sport that he enjoyed more than any other – football.

He'd started playing at the age of six and had quickly fallen in love with it. Football was fast-paced and required physical and mental skill.

But it wasn't just playing it that he loved – he enjoyed watching his friends play too. He'd direct their play, telling them where to go and when to run.

Jürgen couldn't get enough of it.

But Norbert had always said, "Even if you want to be a footballer, it's good to be versatile. Everything will teach you something."

That was why Jürgen was now wrapped in a scarf, gloves, thick boots and four layers of clothing, marching through the snow with a pair of heavy skis over his shoulder.

"So, do you think you want to be a footballer, then?" Norbert asked him, as they continued their climb.

"It could be a career," his dad continued, "but it's a tough one. There's a lot of people out there who want to make it. A lot of pressure if you want to be a footballer."

Jürgen turned to look at his father.

"But to be honest, Jürgen," Norbert added, reading the expression on his son's face, "you don't need to make any decisions right now. You don't even need to be a sportsman! You could be a lawyer, or a teacher, or a doctor … "

"Ooh! I want to be a doctor," Jürgen replied, "I think that would be fun."

"You're not going for anything easy, Jürgen," Norbert laughed. "That's hard work as well."

"Well, I want to do that," Jürgen said again.

Jürgen sighed with relief as they reached the top of the hill. His sisters were already zipping their way down.

"This is a tough one, Jürgen, so take it slow," Norbert said, putting a hand on his son's shoulder. "Don't take any risks."

Jürgen bent down, putting on his skis. Isolde and Stefanie were rapidly disappearing into the distance. It was going to be difficult for him to make it down this hill. He would have to use everything he'd learned on the smaller hills.

He took a deep breath. He'd never been afraid of taking risks. That wasn't going to change now.

"You ready, Jürgen?" Norbert asked.

"Ready," Jürgen replied.

He pushed his skis into the snow and set off down the hill, the wind whistling in his ears.

As he sailed down the hill, he was still thinking about what his father had said. Doctor or footballer. The choices were difficult. But, either way, he was going to make it as one or the other.

3
THE TRIAL

August 1986, Eintracht Frankfurt Training Ground,
Frankfurt, Germany

"I really hope this football thing works out, Jürgen. Because otherwise I think it's not looking good for you."

That's what Jürgen's headteacher had told him when he'd received his higher education exam results. Jürgen had realised early on that he didn't have the brains to become a doctor.

He was a hard worker – he knew exactly what to

study and what he needed to know. But he just couldn't quite make it happen in exams.

It was the same with football. He knew what he wanted to do, but most of the time his body couldn't make it happen. The ball would skew off to the side of the pitch, or he'd go to dribble past someone and the ball would get stuck to his feet. Usually he'd trip over it.

He'd wanted to be a ball-playing midfielder, spraying passes and dribbling through the opposition, but he wasn't suited to it. Instead, because he was tall and physically powerful, he was often used as a striker.

The ball would be sent up to him and he would shrug off defenders and direct it towards his team-mates, who would be swarming around him. Jürgen was a useful addition to any team, but he was never going to be the man that a team was built around.

"Are you sure that you still want to focus on a football career?" his dad had asked him.

The truth was that Jürgen wasn't sure. He'd put everything into becoming a footballer or a doctor. Those had been his two dreams. And now he was at risk of doing neither.

But even when he wasn't touching the ball on the pitch, even when he was a substitute or a spectator, the game just made sense to him. The positions of the players on the pitch – and what they should be doing – just clicked in his mind. He was fascinated by it.

He could tell his team-mates where to go, and he knew they would get the ball. He just couldn't get his own body to do it.

Despite his struggles, he'd decided to give football one more chance. He'd secured a trial at a big local club – Eintracht Frankfurt.

"All of you are here because you want to be professional footballers," the coach told them. "You all believe you could play for one of Germany's biggest clubs. Today, we are going to see if you're right."

There were enough players at the trial for various matches to be taking place at the same time. During a break in play, Jürgen watched some of the other players.

He was particularly impressed by a player who'd earlier introduced himself as Andreas. He was effortlessly brilliant as he moved through the attacking midfield positions, gliding past players and spraying passes out wide.

He was the best player Jürgen had ever seen.

It was a real wake-up call for Jürgen.

"If that's football, then I'm playing a completely different game," he sighed.

For the rest of the trial, Jürgen couldn't focus. Andreas was on such a different level – there was obviously no way that Jürgen was going to be signed up.

Jürgen had never had an incredible touch, but now, in this trial, his playing was suddenly much worse. Even when he was able to get the ball under control, he couldn't turn and shoot.

Nevertheless, he carried on directing his team. It might not be going right for him, but he could still give instructions to his team-mates on the pitch.

"Marco! Bring the ball out to the right!" Jürgen called, seeing the space. "Lukas, close down their left-back!"

He was effectively acting as the captain, orchestrating his team-mates into better positions.

"You've got a good brain for this," the coach told Jürgen, as he debriefed the players after the games. "You were saying a lot of good things out there."

"A first-division head with fourth-division feet," Jürgen chuckled.

The coach smiled, then quickly looked more serious. "I'm sorry, Jürgen. I know you wanted this," he said. "But it's not going to work out today."

Jürgen sighed. He'd come into the trial feeling confident, sure that he was going to make it as a professional player. Now, having seen the rest of the players, it had become clear he wasn't good enough.

His dream of becoming a footballer was being shelved – alongside his dream of being a doctor.

Now he needed a Plan C.

"There's a course at university," the coach said, catching Jürgen's arm. "Sports Science. It might be something that interests you."

Jürgen nodded. He already had a part-time job – working at a local video rental store. Perhaps heading to university would be better than that.

He wasn't sure what he was going to do with his life, but he had the feeling that football wasn't quite done with him yet. There was still more to come.

4

TAKING THE PLUNGE

August 1995, Mainz 05 Training Ground, Mainz, Germany

Jürgen was studying at university, coaching a Frankfurt junior team and playing for a local amateur side, when opportunity came knocking once more. This time, it wasn't a Bundesliga club – it was Mainz 05, in the second tier of German football.

Mainz approached Jürgen looking for a striker who was big, good in the air, and who had a decent understanding of the game. There would be no trial, no coaches to impress and no boxes to tick.

Jürgen was the perfect fit.

But after his initial heartbreak in professional football, did he now want to abandon the new life he'd started building, only to end up being dropped by Mainz in a few years' time?

Once again, his dad was a wise voice.

"It's a risk, Jürgen, of course it is," Norbert said. "There are no guarantees. You could just as easily be unemployed in six months."

"True – but even the second division is professional. It's still a career," Jürgen replied.

"There'd be no safety net, Jürgen. Can you handle that?"

Jürgen thought back to his childhood and that day he'd skied down the hill with his dad and his sisters. It had only been a small hill, but at the time it had felt like a mountain. He'd stood at the top of that hill, knowing the risks, and he'd gone for it. It had made him feel alive.

He knew he had to take this risk.

When he told his dad of his decision, Norbert just smiled wryly.

"What took you so long?"

Jürgen went on to spend five incredible years at Mainz, experiencing both glorious victories and devastating defeats. For all the studying he'd done at university, there was nothing quite like learning on the job.

But as he approached his sixth season with Mainz, the manager, Horst Franz, approached him.

"I know you're a striker, Jürgen," he told him, "and you love scoring goals. But now I want to move you – I want you to be a defender."

Jürgen looked up in surprise.

"I know, I know," Horst nodded, "but you're built perfectly for it. I've seen you come back and help defend. And you can dictate to people and influence the match far more from there than you can from up front."

Jürgen nodded. "That's fine," he said. "I was never that good as a striker anyway."

It was more to learn, but he didn't mind. He already had one eye on the end of his career. He was already studying for his coaching badges and learning how to be a manager. Maybe *that* was what all this was building up to.

5
SURVIVAL

February 2001, Stadion am Bruchweg, Mainz, Germany
Bundesliga 2, Mainz v Duisburg

"The fans love you," Harald Strutz, Mainz's president, had told him. "The players do too. You're brilliant."

"What's going on?" Jürgen had asked, interrupting Strutz's flow. "Who's the new manager? The guys need someone out there. We need a gaffer."

Mainz had been struggling in Bundesliga 2. They'd been through a series of managers – and the latest,

Eckhard Krautzun, had been under intense pressure. There were rumours that he was going to lose his job.

But who would replace him? There was a conveyor belt of German managers who'd been working around Bundesliga 2, but Mainz had already been through most of them.

It was then that the club president, Harald Strutz, had called Jürgen into his office.

"Look, Jürgen," Strutz had begun. "You've been doing your badges. And you've got the passion and intensity that we need in the coming months. So how about it?"

"You don't want someone with more experience?" Jürgen had asked, caught off-guard by the job offer.

We've had lots of experienced managers come through our doors," Strutz had continued. "None of them have captured the players' attention like you."

"Is that enough?" Jürgen had asked. He'd read a lot about tactics, but he didn't know if just being passionate and enthusiastic was enough.

"It's February," Strutz had sighed. "There are seven games until the end of the season. There's no time to change the way we're playing. We need the guys believing. It doesn't matter if it's 4-4-2 or 4-3-3 – we need you to save our season."

And now the day had come – Jürgen's first game as manager, the first of the seven remaining games.

"So those years of going half-way across the country to read books paid off, then?" former team-mate Peter Neustädter asked, slumping down on the dressing room bench next to Jürgen and flashing him a smile.

Towards the end of his playing career with Mainz, Jürgen had been making weekly trips to Cologne, to study with Erich Rutemöller, the Germany assistant manager. Jürgen had wanted to ensure that, when he finished his playing career, he would be in the best position to carry on in football with a coaching career.

He remembered failing at his first trial with Frankfurt. He wasn't going to let that happen again.

"So, are you ready?" Peter asked, looking at his friend.

Jürgen nodded. He hadn't made too many tactical tweaks, sticking with the same players in a 4-4-2. He just needed to say the right things to motivate them.

"There's seven games left this season," he began.

"Seven cup finals. Seven games that are more important than any game that has come before. We win today, and we set ourselves up for survival."

He paused and looked around the room, trying to work out whether everybody was up for this fight.

"Don't do this for me. Don't play for the money, or for your career. Do it for the fans out there. They've turned up for the past six months. Now give them something to cheer."

As the players left the dressing room, Jürgen grabbed Christof Babatz, one of his wingers.

"There's space for you out there, Christof," Jürgen told him. "Don't worry about tracking back. The full-back will push on and leave a big gap. Use it."

Ninety gruelling minutes later, Jürgen was sitting in the dressing room, basking in the glory of a 1-0 win. Just as he'd predicted, it was Babatz who'd grabbed the winner.

Jürgen looked up to see Peter Neustädter standing in front of him.

"One game, one win," Peter grinned. "It's not so hard, this management stuff, is it?"

6
THE CARNIVAL COMES TO TOWN

May 2004, Stadion am Bruchweg, Mainz, Germany
Bundesliga 2, Mainz v Eintracht Trier

"We want to run – we want to run and run. If a single person leaves this stadium at the end of the day thinking they should have run more – then we've not done our job."

Jürgen stood in front of his latest Mainz squad, laying out his plans for the season ahead. Now, he was a long way from the nervous former player who'd taken over the squad in 2001. Back then, he hadn't really had a clue what he'd been doing. He'd set up a basic 4-4-2, reintroducing players who'd been isolated by the former manager.

It hadn't been pretty or technical, but it had been effective. They'd won six of their final seven games, to secure survival with a match to spare.

Three thousand fans had travelled to watch their final game, away at Mannheim. They'd been soundly beaten 4-0 but, as Jürgen and the fans travelled back down the River Rhine on a passenger ship, the planned party went ahead anyway.

Jürgen had been sitting on the boat alongside the Mainz sporting director, Christian Heidel, a man he'd been working closely with. Jürgen was almost a shoo-in for the permanent job now.

The question was, what was next? There was no huge budget for transfers, but Jürgen had faith in his squad.

"Promotion," he'd told Heidel firmly. "That's got to be the target."

Heidel had laughed. "Mainz? The Bundesliga? Those two things just don't go together."

In their entire history, Mainz had never made it to the top level of German football. But Jürgen believed.

"We need a style of play," he'd insisted. "Something simple. Something exciting. Heavy Metal Football!"

That was the phrase that Jürgen had come up with, as they'd sailed down the Rhine. That was the phrase that would stick with him.

He wanted something explosive and fast-paced, something that the players could learn from and improve on over the course of the season.

Jürgen knew from personal experience that not every player could play an eye-of-the-needle pass, or fire a shot into the top corner from 30 yards. But every player could work hard. Every player could run.

He'd set to work, using unorthodox training techniques to keep the players engaged. In shooting drills, he'd set up small walls around the penalty area, so that the ball would rebound unpredictably. Then, wanting his strikers to be first to the second balls, he'd drilled them to react quickly to the bounce.

In his first full season, he'd guided Mainz from fourteenth to fourth. It was impressive, but they'd missed out on promotion by a single place. In his next season, they'd finished fourth again, again narrowly missing promotion.

The dream of getting into the Bundesliga seemed as distant as ever.

At the end of that season, Jürgen had stood in front of 10,000 Mainz fans in the city centre.

"We will get promotion, even after such pain," he'd told them. "We will do what nobody believes we can. So I'm asking you to join us for our first training session of the new season. Give us your support – and we will reward you."

And so, for Mainz's first training session of the new season, thousands of fans had filled the training ground. Such unwavering support was a huge boost to the team's morale.

Now, almost a year later, Mainz were in third place, on the brink of sealing promotion. It was theirs to lose. But they needed to win on the final day of the season – against Eintracht Trier – to be sure of going up.

"We've done the hard yards, boys," Jürgen told the players. "We're an inch from the finish line. We just put one foot in front of the other and we'll seal our place in the Bundesliga. We deserve this. We've earned it."

Manuel Friedrich, Jürgen's trusted assistant, agreed.

"We've done it the right way all season," he added. "We don't do anything different today."

Mainz started the game in their now traditional fashion – fast-paced, hard-working and energetic. They closed down the Trier defence, attempting to win the ball back quickly and not give their opponents a moment on the ball.

"We need an early goal," Jürgen remarked, turning to his right-hand man, Željko Buvač.

"It'll come," Željko replied.

After 20 minutes, the first goal finally did come. Tamás Bódog found Michael Thurk, who finished confidently for his 12th goal of the season.

From then on, Mainz were in cruise control. They added a second goal, and then a third. They were going into the Bundesliga for the first time ever – and Jürgen was the man who was leading them there.

He'd always known that he had a brain for football. His feet had let him down, but his team hadn't.

They'd done the business. Now they were going up.

7
FAIR PLAY

September 2005, Commerzbank-Arena, Frankfurt, Germany
UEFA Cup First Round, Second Leg, Mainz v Sevilla

"We don't play serenity football here," Jürgen told the players. "We don't pass and pass, or run from the challenge. We play the proper stuff. Rainy day, heavy pitch, everybody is muddy, and you go home feeling like you can't play again for weeks."

Mainz were the smallest club in the Bundesliga, with one of the smallest stadiums and the lowest budget.

Most of the pundits had already tipped them to be relegated immediately. Jürgen would have his work cut out if he was going to keep the club afloat.

He didn't have the money for expensive signings, but he was able to snag a couple of free transfers in Conor Casey and Ranisav Jovanović. He wanted players who'd been released by the bigger clubs and were adrift in their careers, with no real clue of where to go next. At Mainz, they could play for a club with a great atmosphere, in front of fans who just loved watching football.

He was using what Mainz did have – passionate fans and eager players – to make up for their lack of money. This was Jürgen's Heavy Metal Football in full effect.

Mainz were taking on some of the Bundesliga's best – and coming out on top. There were heavy defeats as well, but Jürgen knew that losses would happen. His brand of football was as exciting as it was risky.

At the end of the season, they finished comfortably in 11th position. There was also more good news to come.

"We've done it," Željko Buvač announced, bursting into Jürgen's office. "The UEFA Cup. European football!"

"What? How?" Jürgen asked, giving his friend a quizzical look. "We finished eleventh."

"The fair play rules," Željko continued, waving a piece of paper as he spelled it out. Each year, three extra positions in the UEFA Cup were given to the leagues that had been the fairest. The Bundesliga had earned a spot that season, with Mainz being named its fairest team. And so, against the odds, they would be competing against some of Europe's best teams.

Jürgen couldn't wait for the challenge.

Their home games had to be moved to the Commerzbank-Arena in Frankfurt, to meet UEFA regulations for stadium size. Twenty-two thousand fans were crammed inside the arena to watch Mainz breeze through the qualifying rounds, first against Armenian side Mika and then the Icelandic team Keflavík.

Next, they faced the daunting challenge of Sevilla – experienced European competitors with skill, pace and quality. The first leg in Spain ended 0-0, setting up a winner-takes-all home match.

There were over 30,000 fans in the stadium for this game – no doubt the hardest test Jürgen had ever faced.

Jürgen had never devoted that much time to tactics, but the Sevilla team was full of class.

"We can't match them for quality," Jürgen said. "But if we press high and shut down the space, we might just have a chance."

As the players emerged from the tunnel, the atmosphere inside the arena was electric. Jürgen took up his place on the touchline, feeling both excitement and nerves.

Just nine minutes into the match, Frédéric Kanouté gave Sevilla the opener. Then he doubled their lead.

The match was over by half-time. Mainz would have to score three in the second half – and Jürgen knew already that the game was up.

After the final whistle, he trudged back to the dressing room and slumped onto the bench.

He'd never felt so helpless against an opponent before. He'd tried to demonstrate his Heavy Metal Football on the European stage, but he'd been overwhelmingly outplayed.

If Mainz were going to compete in Europe again, he had a lot of work to do.

8
GOOD LUCK

May 2008, Mainz Training Ground, Mainz, Germany

"I think you know why I asked for this meeting," Jürgen said, blinking away the tears that were beginning to appear.

"Jürgen … " Strutz began.

"Last year was tough. Really tough," Jürgen interrupted. "I really thought we could come back."

"We can," Heidel added, "if we can get a couple of signings to strengthen the midfield."

Jürgen was sitting opposite the Mainz management board. Harald Strutz and Christian Heidel were both there, together with other important club staff.

It seemed a lifetime ago that they'd been competing with Sevilla in the UEFA Cup. How had it come to this?

Jürgen's tactics had guided Mainz to a second consecutive eleventh place finish in the Bundesliga. It had looked as if they were set to go up another gear, by qualifying for Europe based on their place in the league. But it hadn't happened.

Instead, Mainz were relegated. And, in large part, it was due to Jürgen's refusal to change tactics. His style of football had brought him success, and he had insisted on sticking to it – even though some of his assistants, players and fans had been calling for change.

No doubt, Jürgen's refusal to compromise had in part led to Mainz's relegation. And, despite his best efforts, Jürgen hadn't been able to get them promoted again the following season.

Despite Mainz's relegation, Jürgen had captured the attention of Germany's biggest clubs. His unique style of pressing football would have enormous potential at a club with the resources to support it. There had been rumours about him joining Schalke, Bayern Munich or Dortmund.

But Jürgen had wanted to stay at Mainz. He'd wanted to do the impossible again and get them promoted back to the Bundesliga.

Then, in heartbreaking fashion, they'd ended the 2007-08 season just two points short of a promotion place.

This crushing failure to get promoted again had taken a heavy toll on Jürgen. Now he knew that he couldn't get the team back to the Bundesliga by playing his style of football.

He knew he was at the end of the road with Mainz.

That was why Jürgen had called a meeting with the Mainz board. He knew they wanted him to stay with the club, and he knew that the players and fans wanted him to stay too.

But he couldn't.

Jürgen choked on his words as he told the Mainz board, "New signings will be for a new manager."

The room fell silent.

"I've always believed in our style of play," he told them, "but I don't know if it's the right fit for Mainz anymore. I don't know if it will get us to where we need to be."

He paused.

"The players are tired. *I'm* tired. I think we all need a change."

The silence sat heavily in the room. Jürgen sensed that they were desperate to talk him out of it, desperate to keep him at the club.

Finally, Harald Strutz spoke.

"Jürgen, you've achieved more at this club than any manager in our history. You've earned the right to choose your future – even if that's away from here."

He sighed. "We wish you all the best. I am sure we will meet again. And when we do, I know you'll have achieved great things."

Another second of silence.

"Good luck."

9
THE YELLOW WALL

September 2008, Signal Iduna Park, Dortmund, Germany
Bundesliga, Dortmund v Schalke

"Welcome to Dortmund, Jürgen." The President of Borussia Dortmund, Reinhard Rauball, shook Jürgen's hand warmly.

"I can't wait to get started," Jürgen replied.

After his departure from Mainz, a number of clubs had expressed an interest in Jürgen, but he had his own criteria for clubs that he would consider joining.

There had been rumours of interest from clubs outside Germany, but Jürgen hadn't yet felt ready to take such a big step.

He'd wanted a club that was like Mainz – under-achievers with a passionate fan base and some good young players, with the potential to build.

Of all the clubs that had made offers, for Jürgen there'd only been one clear option.

Borussia Dortmund.

They'd won the Champions League in the '90s and were one of Germany's biggest clubs. But recently, they'd fallen on hard times.

Last season, they'd finished 13th. For a club of Dortmund's size, that was unacceptable.

They were the perfect club for Jürgen to develop his Heavy Metal Football, so the decision to join them had been a no-brainer.

They regularly attracted around 80,000 fans to their stadium. Jürgen knew the impact that a huge fan base could have, and the size of Dortmund's support dwarfed that at Mainz.

The first thing Jürgen did as Dortmund manager was

controversial. He hadn't yet earned the trust of the fans or the board, but nonetheless he was keen to stamp his authority on the club.

So last season's top-scorer, Mladen Petrić, was out.

Over the years, Jürgen and his assistant, Željko, had seen a lot of Petrić.

"He's a good goalscorer," Željko said, "but he's not the quickest."

"We need a lot of pace up front," Jürgen replied.

So Jürgen sold him, as part of an exchange deal which brought Mohamed Zidan to the club. Jürgen had worked with Zidan before, at Mainz. He matched Jürgen's hard-working style of play exactly.

The next piece of his puzzle was strengthening Dortmund's defence. Jürgen wanted some big, strong central defenders – players who'd put everything on the line to win matches.

They already had Mats Hummels, a young centre-back currently on loan from Bayern Munich, who was likely to join Dortmund permanently.

But Jürgen wanted more. He knew that Dortmund didn't have the budget to spend 20 or 30 million on a player, but he knew that there were some bargains out there.

In the end, he went back to what he knew best – his old club, Mainz. Last summer, they'd acquired a young Serbian centre-back, Neven Subotić, who'd quickly become a mainstay in the team. He was strong and quick, and had quality on the ball.

He became the next man to join the revolution that Jürgen was leading at Dortmund.

"I'm not saying we're going to make the top six," Jürgen told his players before the season began. "But we need to be taking steps to get us to the place where this club belongs. Are we going to win the league in May? Probably not. But in two or three years?"

He shrugged, leaving the question open. This was a club that should be competing for the top trophies. And he wanted to be the man to lead them there.

They started the season well, with two wins away from home and a hard-fought draw with Bayern Munich.

But the next match was the big one. Jürgen was well aware of the importance of Borussia Dortmund v

Schalke. It was one of the biggest derbies in football – bigger than anything he'd encountered at Mainz.

On top of that, Schalke were currently top of the league, the big guns in the Bundesliga. This would be a real test for his new team, and Dortmund needed to show that they could deliver.

Jürgen went for the 4-4-2 that had served him so well during his time at Mainz. He also avoided giving his players too much of a pep-talk before the game. For a Dortmund player, this was *the* derby – the ultimate game in German football. They shouldn't need a manager's talk to get them motivated.

But at half-time, the players trudged back in, 2-0 down. Perhaps Jürgen had misjudged it. Worse, the fans – who were going to be such an important part of Dortmund's season – had already turned on them.

The confidence of the players was hanging by a thread.

"We're better than this, guys," Jürgen told them. "We're playing like amateurs, like this is a Saturday in the park. This is Schalke. We're Dortmund. There are 80,000 fans out there, here to see us. Even if we don't win, let's give them some moments that they can talk about. Even if we lose, we have to fight."

He thought he'd said the right things and, looking around, the players seemed to be motivated. But in the second half, they quickly fell behind by a third goal.

He'd already thrown on Alex Frei and Diego Klimowicz and, without any more options on the bench, now it would have to be the players already out there.

Ten minutes later, Dortmund pulled a goal back, when a delicious corner from Frei was headed home by Neven Subotić. The fans were starting to turn Dortmund's way now, as the players pressed hard for another goal.

Jürgen was urging his players on from the sidelines, imagining himself kicking every ball that was played.

A moment later, the two substitutes combined as Tinga flicked the ball into Frei, who whipped home from distance. 3-2!

Now both the fans and the players were starting to believe. Now Schalke were the ones on the back foot.

Then, in the space of five minutes, Dortmund's opponents were down to nine men, as a result of two red cards. Now Jürgen didn't just want to draw. He wanted to win.

Rattled, Schalke shut up shop and started defending for their lives. Dortmund couldn't find a way through.

"Come on, boys!" Jürgen bellowed, all sense of tactics gone out of the window. There was nothing more to say.

In the last minute, a shot was blocked by the arm of a Schalke defender. There was only one option.

Penalty.

Alex Frei, the man who'd come on and rescued the game, was Dortmund's penalty-taker. Their captain, Sebastian Kehl, came running over to Frei.

"Don't get carried away, Alex," Kehl told him. "Keep cool. The keeper will panic – this is your moment."

Frei stepped up and smashed it low into the bottom-left corner. The keeper had panicked and dived the wrong way, just as Kehl had predicted.

Dortmund had come from 3-0 down to claim a draw in the Revierderby. The fans had now been introduced to Jürgen's football – and they were loving it.

They couldn't wait for the rest of the season.

IO
UNTOUCHABLE

February 2011, Allianz Arena, Munich, Germany
Bundesliga, Bayern Munich v Dortmund

"We're finally into Europe." Jürgen smiled.

"Thirteenth, to sixth, to fifth. It's been constant improvement since you joined us, Jürgen," Hans-Joachim Watzke, Dortmund's boss, told him, sitting across the table. "Champions League next?"

Jürgen shrugged. He knew that the question wasn't serious – there was no real insistence that Dortmund qualify for the Champions League. Jürgen had his own personal aims for the season, and he knew that they differed from Watzke's.

The fans and the board simply wanted to enjoy their time in Europe. But Jürgen wanted more.

Over the past two years, he'd been building the side that he hoped would get him there. Dortmund got the best results when they were going at teams at a breakneck pace – and that's exactly what Jürgen had built his team around.

He introduced younger players from the academy – players who had the energy to maintain his style of play. They sometimes made mistakes, and they weren't always composed or mature, but they believed in the way that Jürgen wanted his team to play.

Two academy graduates, Mario Götze and Kevin Großkreutz, joined the ranks. They were then joined by Łukasz Piszczek from Hertha Berlin, Shinji Kagawa from Cerezo Osaka, and Nuri Şahin, who had returned from a loan at Feyenoord.

Jürgen's additions were capped off with a little-known striker from Lech Poznań – Robert Lewandowski.

The season got off to a flying start.

By Christmas, Dortmund weren't just top of the table – they were several points clear and running away with it. Schalke, Leverkusen and Bayern were all falling behind. Jürgen's unorthodox squad was working wonders.

Jürgen knew that there was a long way to go in the season. He may not have won the Bundesliga before, but he had achieved promotion, and it was the same principle. You had to be at 100% all through the season.

Dortmund's poor performances were limited to the cup competitions and, although they were eliminated from the DFB-Pokal and the Europa League early on, this simply focused their minds more closely on the Bundesliga.

Their form dipped at the beginning of 2011, but going into a match against their big rivals, Bayern Munich, they were 13 points clear of the reigning champions.

For this game, Jürgen was without experienced goalkeeper and captain Roman Weidenfeller, due to injury. This meant that he was forced into handing a debut to the young keeper Mitchell Langerak.

It also meant that Dortmund were fielding the

youngest team in Bundesliga history – and against the mighty Bayern at that.

"We haven't won here … in Munich … for almost 20 years," Jürgen told them, making the pauses count. The players needed to understand the importance of today's game.

"But today, we come here as favourites," he continued. "We come here as *the* big team in Germany. Last season, Bayern won the double. This year, we are 13 points clear. Let's knock them out of the title race with a win."

Lewandowski was playing behind the prolific Barrios. Großkreutz lined up on the left, with his relentless energy meaning he'd effectively be playing as a fifth defender. And on the right, Mario Götze was a constant threat.

It was a team built to make history.

There was a thrilling atmosphere inside the Allianz Arena. Despite their place in the table, the Bayern fans still believed that they could catch Dortmund.

They were quickly silenced.

Großkreutz won the ball off a sloppy Bayern pass and drove forward. He then played the ball to Lucas Barrios, who poked it past Thomas Kraft.

Dortmund had the lead.

It didn't take long for more goals to come.

First, Luiz Gustavo volleyed Bayern level. Then, three minutes later, Dortmund were back in front. Nuri Şahin, captain for the day, picked the ball up outside the box and curled it into the top corner.

"Bayern are going to come at us," Jürgen told his players at half-time. "We'll need to weather the storm. Let's show them our resilience."

The players did more than that. Fifteen minutes into the second half, Mats Hummels headed them further ahead.

This time, there was no way back for Bayern.

Dortmund had won. They had won in Munich for the first time in 19 years, going 16 points clear of their arch-rivals.

They already had one hand on the Bundesliga trophy. They were untouchable.

II
MONEY TALKS

May 2012, Olympiastadion, Berlin, Germany
DFB-Pokal Final, Dortmund v Bayern Munich

" 'Borussia Dortmund are Champions of Germany!' "
Jürgen read the newspaper headline aloud. "Sounds
good. Right, Željko?"

Jürgen and Željko were sitting in Jürgen's office, after
returning from their end-of-season break. They'd won
the 2010-11 Bundesliga title by seven points, finally
putting Dortmund back at the top of German football.

"It does," replied Željko. "And now it's time to do it all over again! We've got the Champions League this year too, so we'll need squad depth."

"We've got the academy," Jürgen reminded him. He was reluctant to buy new players when there were young prospects waiting for their chance.

Jürgen didn't want to disrupt a winning side. He held his nerve in the transfer market, only dipping in for a couple of major purchases. After Nuri Şahin was poached by Spanish giants Real Madrid, Jürgen swiftly moved to replace him with the young German midfielder, İlkay Gündoğan.

He also added strength in attack, with the arrival of pacy Croatian winger Ivan Perišić. Once more, he was adding youth and creativity to his team, without breaking the bank.

For all the changes and preparations, their Champions League group was a tough one, and it was immediately clear that they could not compete. Heavy defeats to Marseille and Olympiacos left them bottom of the group and out of Europe. Jürgen knew he would need a different plan for European football.

For the first time in his career, Jürgen was forced to consider altering his tactics. Perhaps in Europe they could be more solid defensively. Despite always having used a 4-4-2 or a 4-2-3-1, he began to consider moving towards the more controlled 4-3-3.

But, for now, he had to turn his attention back to the Bundesliga. After a rocky start, Dortmund were once again top of the table. There were big wins over Cologne, Wolfsburg and Hamburg, as well as a crucial win over Bayern Munich.

And they were being pushed on by their new star, Robert Lewandowski. Robert had struggled during his first season at Dortmund, often playing second fiddle to the in-form Lucas Barrios. In fact, he hadn't even reached double figures in goals.

But Jürgen had been undeterred.

"Let's make it interesting," Jürgen had suggested to Lewandowski. "If you score ten goals in training, I will give you 50 euros. If you don't, you pay me."

For most of the previous season, Jürgen had been raking in the cash. Lewandowski had been struggling, with every shot being skewed wide. And at the end of every session, he would reach into his bag, fish out his wallet and hand a crumpled note to his boss.

But as the 2011-12 season had progressed, Jürgen had gradually found himself to be the one reaching into his wallet most often. Every touch had turned into a goal, and every pass had been crisp and precise.

It hadn't just been in training either. Robert had begun to turn it on in matches too. He'd become Dortmund's main striker and, halfway through the season, Jürgen had had to end their little arrangement.

"Enough!" Jürgen had said to Lewandowski at the end of training one day, his palm outstretched. "I can't afford this, Lewa! You win!"

Jürgen had pretended outrage but, on the inside, he'd been beaming. He had a striker who was now scoring 30 goals a season – and it had barely cost him a thing. He'd spent more on their little bets than he had on the striker.

With Lewandowski in the form of his life and Mario Götze, Błaszczykowski and Kagawa behind him, Dortmund had gone the rest of the season unbeaten, smashing several Bundesliga records as they sealed a second consecutive title.

But there had also been another trophy on the line, in the final of the DFB-Pokal – against their toughest opponents, Bayern Munich.

Jürgen made just one change to his squad, benching Mario Götze and selecting the hardworking trio of Kagawa, Błaszczykowski and Großkreutz behind Lewandowski.

The game itself was everything that Jürgen believed football should be. His side burst into an early lead, after a mistake at the back allowed Błaszczykowski to square for Kagawa to tap home.

Bayern equalised through a penalty, before Dortmund hit back with a penalty of their own, converted by Hummels.

And then Lewandowski took over. An instinctive right-footed finish. A rifled strike into the far corner. And finally, a bullet-header from close range. He scored a sensational hat-trick to seal a 5-2 win for Dortmund.

They had outrun, outworked and outplayed Bayern. Jürgen had won Dortmund's first-ever league and cup double, outwitting the biggest team in Germany, on just a fraction of their budget.

From here, the only way was up.

12
ALL-OUT ATTACK

April 2013, Signal Iduna Park, Dortmund, Germany
Champions League Semi-Final, Dortmund v Real Madrid

There was no doubt – Jürgen had totally conquered domestic football in Germany. He'd won it all, sweeping aside every club that had stood in his way.

He'd established himself as one of the best managers in Europe, and had received offers from many other clubs. But he'd dismissed them all. He had unfinished business with Dortmund in Europe.

Jürgen dipped into the market once more, bringing in exciting young winger Marco Reus to replace Shinji Kagawa, who'd left for Man United.

Then he quickly set about adapting his team for the Champions League.

"It's slower," Jürgen said to Željko. "The referees are quicker to blow up for a foul – we have to be more cautious."

"I'm not sure we do," Željko countered. "Maybe before. But Hummels and Gündoğan are world-class now, and Lewa is probably the best striker in the world."

Jürgen frowned. He'd stuck to his guns in European football before and it had brought him disappointment. He didn't want it to happen again.

His focus on European football came with a slight slip in their domestic form. Dortmund weren't playing badly, but Bayern, under newly-appointed Pep Guardiola, had improved dramatically.

Jürgen had set his sights on qualifying from their group in the Champions League – and it had worked. They'd beaten the English and Spanish champions, in Man City and Real Madrid, to finish top of the group.

And it had all come from playing football the way Jürgen wanted it played. He'd taken Željko's advice and gone for it, playing all his big guns and encouraging his team to attack.

Teams were surprised by the way Dortmund were playing – that wasn't the way it was usually done in the Champions League.

After battling through exciting knockout stages, Dortmund found themselves in a mouth-watering semi-final against Real Madrid.

Jürgen was well-prepared for this game. Not only had they played Real Madrid twice in the group stages, but he had meticulously studied all their games over the past season. He'd also analysed their manager – José Mourinho.

Mourinho was the exact opposite of Jürgen. He was defensively-minded and cynical, preferring to play football a different way.

"We know what their weaknesses are," Jürgen told his team. "They're a team of individuals. They have brilliant players, but they are not a team."

"They won't work as hard as us," İlkay Gündoğan added. "Nobody does."

The one big concern for them was Cristiano Ronaldo. Jürgen could account for most things in football, but he couldn't counter one of the best players in the world.

"Don't focus on him," Jürgen told Piszczek, who'd have the task of marking the forward. "If he scores, he scores. Treat him like any other player."

"Remember," Željko added, "he won't track back. You'll have space going forward. Use it. Don't worry about leaving him unmarked."

There was a brilliant atmosphere inside the stadium for the first leg. The yellow wall was in full swing and the noise coming from the fans was deafening.

"I wouldn't want to be a Madrid player," Jürgen remarked, as they exited the tunnel and took their seats.

It didn't take long for the first goal. Once more, it was Lewandowski, poking home from close range. Dortmund had the lead.

The Real Madrid response came almost single-handedly from Ronaldo, tapping the ball into an open net after a ruthless counter-attack. It was 1-1.

"Focus, boys," Jürgen insisted. "Keep going. Keep playing!"

Most managers would want cool heads during a game of this magnitude. But Jürgen wanted his players fired up. He wanted them playing his way.

At half-time, the score was still 1-1.

"We can take them," Jürgen told his players. "We can beat them."

He didn't say any more – no new tactics, no changes.

Lewandowski got his second goal early in the second half. Then he rifled home a brilliant third and, ten minutes later, added a penalty to seal the game at 4-1.

At full time, Jürgen pumped his fist in the air, before going over to shake the hand of José Mourinho, a man who'd won the Champions League just three years earlier.

"You deserved that, Jürgen," José said, his face expressionless. "That was brilliant."

That was the great José Mourinho – the man who'd won multiple European titles. And Jürgen had beaten him. And more than that, he was now just one game away from a Champions League final.

13
THE END OF AN ERA

May 2013, Wembley Stadium, London, England
Champions League Final, Dortmund v Bayern Munich

"So, Mario's going," Željko announced.

The words that Jürgen had hoped he would never have to hear had been uttered to him just a few days before the second leg of a Champions League semi-final.

Mario Götze, Dortmund's home-grown talisman and superstar, had announced that he would be leaving the club to join their arch-rivals, Bayern Munich.

"That's the way it is, Jürgen," Željko had told him. "We just can't compete with what they're offering."

"How can that be true?" Jürgen protested. "We've won the league two years running – we won the double. We're on the verge of a Champions League final!"

But Željko was right. In football, money talked. History talked. Dortmund may have won the last two titles, but Bayern were way clear this season, smashing all the records that Dortmund had set just a year earlier.

They'd also knocked Dortmund out of the DFB-Pokal. And now, the giants from Bavaria stood between Dortmund and their second Champions League title.

It was the first time ever that there had been an all-German Champions League final.

"It's just not right," Mats Hummels complained. "Mario tells us he's going to leave. They beat us in the league and the cup – and now here they are again!"

"Remember, guys," Jürgen reminded them. "We beat them twice last year. And they lost this final. These things go both ways."

But privately, Jürgen was equally annoyed.

"Why did Mario have to tell us on the eve of the final

that he was leaving for Bayern?" he complained to Željko. "What does that do for morale? What does that say?"

"At least he's injured," Željko shrugged. "Avoids us having to choose whether to play him."

"But we need him," Jürgen replied. "Look at this Bayern team. Look at the bench alone! They could change their whole starting eleven and still have a line-up to win the Bundesliga."

"We've beaten them before," Željko added. "Same tactics … "

"They'll expect that," Jürgen said. "We need something more."

His options were limited, but he had the addition of their new exciting attacker, Marco Reus, to play in the number 10 role, behind Lewandowski. And, once more, he turned to the boundless energy of Kevin Großkreutz on the left and Jakub Błaszczykowski on the right.

"Robben and Ribéry are the threat," he told his wingers, in the build-up to the game. "But they won't help their full-backs. Press high, early on. Make them play the ball and force the mistakes."

"Lewa," he said, calling his striker over. "You'll

probably have a quiet game, so you'll have to be ready to strike when the ball breaks your way. Be ruthless."

Jürgen gathered the rest of his team around him.

"There will be no surprises today, boys," he said. "We know who we're playing. We know what they're good at and what they're bad at. And they know the same about us. This is the last game of our season. One last push. Make yourselves legends. There's no point playing at 90%. This is it. Give everything and, even if we lose, we'll know that we did all we could."

Despite the final being played in London, there was still a huge Dortmund presence in the stands. Jürgen didn't know how many fans had made the trip but, for the Dortmund players, it felt like a home game in the stadium. They had that advantage, at least.

Without exchanging words, Jürgen shook hands with the Bayern manager, Jupp Heynckes.

Jürgen had seen enough finals to know that they were usually tense, cagey affairs. But this wasn't the case when Dortmund were involved. As always, they were at their best when they were going full-throttle.

Their start was electric, with Błaszczykowski, Reus

and Lewandowski all forcing Neuer into saves. Within the first 25 minutes, it was clear to see why the Bayern keeper was regarded as one of the best in the world.

But the intensity also left spaces behind Dortmund's defence. Twice, Arjen Robben was almost in, but was denied both times by Weidenfeller. Dortmund's keeper was by now accustomed to his club's style, and he was lightning-quick off his line, constantly blocking Robben's attempts.

"Come on, Roman!" Jürgen roared, cheering his keeper's second huge save.

At half-time, they were still level at 0-0. Once again, Jürgen pushed them on.

"Forty-five minutes between us and glory. Give it everything!"

But Bayern had grown into the game, showing their class and experience. On the hour mark, Robben weaved his way around the defenders, before squaring to Mario Mandžukić, who poked home.

Jürgen now had to think about changes. Who would he bring on? Who *could* he bring on?

His thoughts were interrupted by shouts from the bench around him. Marco Reus had gone down in the box – and the referee was pointing to the spot. Penalty!

"Dante's been booked!" Željko bellowed. "Send him off!"

But it wasn't to be. He stayed on the pitch.

İlkay Gündoğan stepped up to take the penalty. He ran up and slotted it hard to the keeper's left, sending Neuer the wrong way.

"YES!" Jürgen roared, his shouts drowned out by the noise from the Dortmund fans. The game was back on.

Bayern were still coming forward and Subotić was forced into a clearance off the line.

Neither manager was willing to make any changes. Their best players were out there and, anyway, nobody wanted to come into a game being played at this pace.

The game was heading towards extra time when Bayern lifted the ball forward. Ribéry flicked it into Robben, who evaded the desperate lunges of two Dortmund defenders, before shooting past Weidenfeller.

The game was over. Dortmund had lost the Champions League.

Jürgen sat in the Wembley dressing room, unable to lift his players or himself. It felt like the end of an era.

How could they come back from this?

14
A WALK THROUGH TIME

April 2015, Signal Iduna Park, Dortmund, Germany

Jürgen strolled through the halls of Dortmund's famous stadium, glancing at the photographs and trophies that adorned the walls.

Some showed pictures of his most recent triumphs – the first Bundesliga win in 2011, the league and cup double in 2012. Even the Champions League final from 2013 – the first all-German final – had its own photo.

That was the one that Dortmund had come so close to winning.

Jürgen looked at the faces in the photos of earlier title wins. So few of the players were still at the club.

In the summer after the final, Mario Götze had departed for Bayern. Then, in the autumn, Robert Lewandowski had announced that he would be going the same way in the following summer.

The players that remained were now a year older and a step or two slower.

Dortmund were no longer the shocking, vibrant team they had been when Jürgen had first taken over. Now, opponents understood how Dortmund played their game – and they knew what to expect. Dortmund had become predictable.

And whilst Bayern, Leverkusen and Gladbach were getting stronger, Dortmund had lost some of their edge. And now they'd lost two of their best players.

On the plus side, Jürgen now had more money to play with, so he'd signed Henrikh Mkhitaryan, Pierre-Emerick Aubameyang and Ciro Immobile. The new signings found various degrees of success, but ultimately they failed to replicate the successes of those they had replaced.

In the season after their famous Champions League run, Dortmund had finished second – nineteen points behind Pep Guardiola's Bayern Munich team.

It hadn't even been close.

Pep had brought a new style of play to the Bundesliga. Bayern were the pass masters, who smothered teams, preventing them from playing. In many ways, it was the opposite of Jürgen's pressing style.

And Pep had won out. Bayern were now dominant.

The following season had been even worse for Jürgen. Dortmund had lost 11 of their first 20 games and, by the middle of February, they'd found themselves bottom of the table. The prospect of relegation had suddenly seemed very real.

It had taken all of Jürgen's powers of motivation to guide his team to safety.

He'd been able to alter their tactics by moving Aubameyang to the centre and getting Marco Reus back into the starting line-up.

They'd managed to turn it around with several wins

and, in the middle of April, they sat in tenth place, comfortably in mid-table.

By Dortmund's (and Jürgen's own) high standards, this had still been a failure.

Because of all he'd done for the club, the Dortmund board had made it clear that Jürgen wouldn't be sacked. Both the board and the fans continued to support him.

Jürgen knew that the players were still behind him too. He'd brought many of them to the club and had guided them to such unexpected heights.

But as he walked through the halls of the stadium that had borne witness to some of the best moments of his life, Jürgen knew that his time was up.

He simply didn't know how to get Dortmund back to the top. He didn't know how to beat Bayern.

Without knocking, he entered the office of the Dortmund boss, Hans-Joachim Watzke. He didn't need to knock – Watzke knew he was coming. There were no surprises today.

"Can't I change your mind, Jürgen?" Watzke asked, his voice almost cracking as he got straight to business. He knew why Jürgen was there.

"This is an extraordinary club," Jürgen said. "One of the best in the world. I always said that, if a time came when I wasn't the best man to take it forward, I would step down."

"You're still that man," Watzke insisted. "Trust me, you are."

"Not any more," Jürgen replied grimly. "I don't know how to beat them any more."

"We can spend money. Stop them buying our players."

"There's nobody to bring in. Not for me," Jürgen said. "Someone else can maybe take it on. They might be able to get the best from them."

Watzke sighed. They'd worked together for a long time, and he knew Jürgen as well as anyone. And he knew when his manager's mind was made up.

"Where will you go?" he asked.

"I don't know," Jürgen said, his face breaking into the smallest smile, as he felt a great weight lift off his shoulders – for the first time in seven years. "I really don't know."

15
GETTING DEFENSIVE

May 2016, St. Jakob-Park, Basel, Switzerland
Europa League Final, Liverpool v Sevilla

"I didn't think we'd be back in football again so soon. Didn't you want to take any time off?" Željko Buvač, Jürgen's long-time friend and assistant, asked.

"You didn't have to come with me," Jürgen remarked. "You could have had some time off."

"How would you cope without me?" Željko grinned.

It had only been six months since Jürgen had

announced his intention to leave Borussia Dortmund, and four months since his final game – a 3-1 defeat in the DFB-Pokal final to Wolfsburg.

He had been honest with Watzke during their conversation – he genuinely hadn't known what he was going to do when he left Dortmund. But even though he'd been exhausted during his final few months at the club, he hadn't wanted a long break from football.

But he also hadn't spoken to any clubs, and he had no idea who might want him. There'd been interest from Manchester City and Real Madrid but, just as when he'd left Mainz, he'd had his own set of criteria for the kind of club he was willing to join.

City and Real Madrid were both great clubs, with huge amounts of money and resources, and very impressive squads. But neither had what Jürgen had been looking for.

Then, in the October of 2015, a club that ticked all his boxes had approached him. Liverpool.

Just two years ago, they'd gone within a whisker of winning the Premier League, but since then, they'd fallen back on harder times.

They had one of the most famous stadiums and fan bases in Europe, but they'd never won the Premier League. They had a decent squad – but not an incredible one. There was money for transfers, but Jürgen had known it would be a challenge to recruit the players he needed.

And if there was one thing he loved, it was a challenge.

It had been his first job outside of Germany and he'd had to adapt quickly to the Premier League. Football in the Bundesliga had been played at a fast pace, but the Premier League had made it look like a stroll in the park.

Every team was physical and competitive, and every team had at least a few brilliant players. But there was no Bayern Munich – no team that stood head and shoulders above everyone else.

Liverpool had had some good players of their own, including Firmino, Coutinho and Sturridge. But Jürgen had struggled during his first few games. Liverpool had been good going forward, but defensively they'd been vulnerable.

It had been one of Brendan Rodgers' assistants, Pep Lijnders, who'd suggested a change of set-up.

"4-3-3," he'd proposed. "We have Emre Can and Henderson playing holding. Maybe Milner as well. It means Coutinho and Firmino don't have to defend."

He'd been right. Jürgen's regular formation of a 4-2-3-1 or a 4-4-2 wouldn't have been able to cut it with the defensive options he'd had available. There'd been no Mats Hummels or Subotić to mop up the gaps behind his midfield, and no Roman Weidenfeller to come rushing out from goal.

He'd known that he would have to work with what he had.

Gradually, he'd been able to mould the team towards his style, whilst also keeping defensively strong. There'd been big wins away at Chelsea and Man City, but he'd been frustrated by the smaller teams and their defensive approach.

"It's so annoying," he complained to Željko. "In Germany, every team attacks. They come out and play football. They *want* to play."

"But here, they don't, " Željko nodded.

Liverpool had been inconsistent and, as Jürgen gradually adapted to the league, they ultimately finished eighth, outside the Champions League places. There had also been a heart-breaking penalty shootout defeat in the final of the League Cup, against Manchester City.

But that hadn't been their only final. Thanks to dramatic wins over Manchester United and Dortmund, Jürgen's former club, Liverpool had made it to the final of the Europa League.

And it was against Jürgen's old rivals, Sevilla.

"They beat me with Mainz," he moaned. "And they beat me with Dortmund. It's always them."

"That was a long time ago," Željko reminded him. "We're both with very different teams now."

"They're the team who've won this two years in a row," Jürgen frowned.

He was right. This was Sevilla's competition. They'd won it many times, and Liverpool were the team who'd already lost a final this year.

Despite his nerves, Jürgen had gone back to his roots with his team selection for the final. This wasn't the Premier League – here he could be more expansive. Roberto Firmino and Daniel Sturridge lined up together, flanked by the creative duo of Coutinho and Lallana.

There was a lot riding on this game – not just for Liverpool, but for Jürgen as well. This was their last opportunity to get back into the Champions League, as well as his opportunity to stop a run of four consecutive final defeats, stretching back to his time with Dortmund.

He needed this.

And they started superbly, with Daniel Sturridge curling home a brilliant strike in the first half. Liverpool were one up. They'd been denied a penalty, but they were the team on top. All they had to do was hold on.

But in the space of a brutal opening minute to the second half, all their good work was undone.

Mariano got past Moreno too easily on Liverpool's left and squared the ball, to give Kevin Gameiro a simple tap-in. Jürgen saw his players' heads drop. They'd lost all the confidence that had come with the first goal.

Then a quickfire brace from Koke took the game away from Liverpool. Sevilla were 3-1 up and cruising.

There would be no Champions League football for Jürgen next season. In fact, there would be no European football of any kind.

It would be the Prem or nothing. The pressure was on.

16
MOVING FORWARD

May 2017, Anfield, Liverpool, England
Premier League, Liverpool v Middlesbrough

Jürgen's first season outside Germany had finished in disappointment. They'd been soundly beaten by Sevilla in the Europa League final and were a long way adrift of the top four in the Premier League.

There had been work to do at Dortmund and at Mainz when he'd joined them – and it looked as if Liverpool was going to be no different.

In fact, it was probably going to be his biggest challenge yet.

Before the season began, Jürgen gathered together his team of assistants – Željko, Pep Lijnders and Peter Krawietz. These were the guys who had to work out how to get Liverpool back to the top of the table.

"So, 'Heavy Metal Football', boss. What's it all about?" Pep Lijnders asked, as the coaches sat down around the large meeting table. "Why are we always pressing so hard? The players say it's exhausting!"

"If we lose the ball," Jürgen replied with a grin, "we get it back straight away. We don't all pull back and wait for the other team to do something with it. When a player wins the ball off you, he will have taken his eye off the game – he won't know where on the pitch his team-mates are. He's also used energy tackling you. So the moment when he gets the ball is the moment when he's most vulnerable. *That's* when we get it back off him."

Jürgen looked at Peter Krawietz, who'd been with him at Mainz and knew Jürgen's approach very well.

"Yeah, that's Heavy Metal Football in a nutshell," Peter added with a smile.

"OK. So what's our biggest weakness?" Jürgen asked his assistants, looking over his team list. "What do we struggle with?"

There were a couple of nervous glances between the coaches, as they wondered if their manager was asking a genuine question.

"Seriously," Jürgen added.

"Defending," Željko volunteered. "We're vulnerable when teams attack us. If they get in behind our midfield."

"We have a couple of options," Jürgen said. "We can work on defending – bolster our midfield and go after some more defenders."

"Or?" Krawietz asked.

"We lean into it," Jürgen continued. "We go for hard-working, attacking players. We press teams as soon as they get the ball – and defend from the front.'"

"We'll still concede," Željko warned.

"OK, we can add one or two defenders," Jürgen replied. "But if we go into games accepting that we might concede one or two, but knowing we'll score three or four … that's a win."

He could sense that his coaches were unsure. Every

instinct in their body was telling them it was too risky. Better to add a couple of world-class defenders, or play two holding midfielders. But that wasn't Jürgen's style.

He quickly went about rebuilding his Liverpool squad. Out went Kolo Touré, Martin Škrtel, Joe Allen, Christian Benteke and Jordon Ibe. And in came Joël Matip, Loris Karius, Sadio Mané and Georginio Wijnaldum.

Mané was a pacy, dangerous player, as prolific in front of goal as he was hard-working off the ball. On the other hand, Wijnaldum was the ultimate box-to-box midfielder. He'd pop up in both penalty areas, scoring goals at one end and making blocks and tackles at the other.

Jürgen gathered his new squad together before the start of the season.

"Last year was a start," Jürgen told the players. "We had some great games where we were magnificent. We've got no European football this season, which is a good thing for us. It means that we can focus on just one thing – the league. We have one aim."

He held up a single finger.

"We get back into the Champions League. This is

Liverpool football club – we belong in the Champions League."

His captain, Jordan Henderson, got to his feet.

"We want to make sure we win the little games too, guys," he added. "Last season, we were great against the big teams. But this year, every game matters."

Jürgen was already starting to build this team in the same mould as his Dortmund and Mainz teams. He knew there were players here who believed in him.

They began the season with an end-to-end 4-3 win over Arsenal at the Emirates. It summed up everything that Jürgen was trying to achieve with his new team. They conceded three, but they scored four and won.

The season continued with similar wins, as well as the disappointing moments of defeats to Hull and Leicester.

On the final day of the season, Liverpool were in fourth spot – just a point clear of Arsenal. A win at home against Middlesbrough would guarantee them a place in the Champions League.

"We know what we wanted from this season," Jürgen told his players. "Now we're just one game from that. Three points – that's all we need."

James Milner was starting at left-back today, with the midfield trio of Can, Lallana and Wijnaldum supporting the attack. An injury to Sadio Mané meant that Sturridge, Firmino and Coutinho were the front three. It wasn't too far removed from the team that Jürgen had used for most of the last season – but now there was a real confidence about them. They believed.

" 'Boro are already relegated – but don't let that fool you." Milner added. "They will fight for every ball."

It was a nervous start to the match, with the Liverpool players feeling the pressure. This wasn't the Liverpool who'd been playing so well all season.

But that all changed just before half-time, when Georginio Wijnaldum put Liverpool ahead. Coutinho and Lallana then scored a goal each in the second half.

Liverpool had comfortably won the game 3-0. They were back in the Champions League. They'd finished another season without a trophy, but they'd made huge leaps forward.

"One or two additions, that's all we need," Jürgen remarked to Željko, as they celebrated the result. "This is going to be even better than Dortmund. I just know it."

17
A FAMILIAR FACE

April 2018, Anfield, Liverpool, England
Champions League Quarter-Final, Liverpool v Man City

"Do you know what our biggest strength was at Dortmund?" Jürgen turned to his assistant, Pep Lijnders.

"Lewandowski?" Lijnders guessed.

"He helped," Jürgen conceded, rolling his eyes. "But we had the ability to create goals from all areas of the pitch. We had full-backs bursting forward, pacy wingers and creative number 10s."

"You think Liverpool don't have that?" Pep asked.

"We *didn't*," Jürgen said. "We do now."

Liverpool's qualification for the Champions League had enabled big-money arrivals, in the form of Mohamed Salah and Alex Oxlade-Chamberlain. These were players that would have been harder to reach, if the incentive of Champions League football hadn't been there.

But it wasn't those that Jürgen was most excited about. He'd picked up Andrew Robertson, a young Scottish full-back from Hull, for a small fee of just 10 million – a bargain in Premier League terms.

Left-back had been a problem area for Liverpool. James Milner had filled in over the previous season, as Alberto Moreno had been a less than convincing option. At Dortmund, Jürgen had had Łukasz Piszczek and Marcel Schmelzer charging forward from both flanks. He wanted to replicate that at Liverpool.

At right-back, it wasn't a new signing who'd found himself in the team. Jürgen had stumbled upon a young academy prospect by the name of Trent Alexander-Arnold. He'd watched him during training and was struck by his ability to whip in a cross or a free kick.

"That kid," Jürgen had remarked to his assistants. "He's got something special. We need something like that."

It didn't take long for Trent and Robertson to become key cogs in Jürgen's Liverpool team. In midfield, Henderson, Wijnaldum and Emre Can were the trio that enabled Jürgen's team to function as it did.

It had been looking increasingly likely that Philippe Coutinho was going to leave the club, so Jürgen was attempting to replace him before it happened. Rather than finding a direct replacement, he decided to use Roberto Firmino in a new way.

"If Bobby Firmino drops in, he can basically play like a number 10," Jürgen said, moving the little magnets around on his tactics board.

"That creates the space for Sadio and Mo," Pep added. "Has Bobby got that ability?"

Jürgen looked at him and raised an eyebrow.

"Of course he has," he laughed. "The question is, can Mo and Sadio finish the chances he makes? They'll have space to run into, and they'll have Trent and Robbo on the overlap. Wijnaldum will be coming through as well."

Jürgen clapped his hands together, grinning broadly.

His team was almost perfect. He couldn't wait to see it in action.

He'd expected the results to be good, but even he was surprised by the speed with which Mo Salah took to the Premier League. The young Egyptian had previously been disappointing for Chelsea, but it was now obvious that he'd changed a lot since then. He simply couldn't stop scoring.

There was the odd disappointing result, such as a 5-0 defeat at Man City – not helped by Sadio Mané's early red card – but overall, Liverpool were in brilliant form.

They'd stormed through their Champions League group, scoring 23 goals (including two separate 7-0 wins). Then, in the last 16, they'd thrashed Porto 5-0. And now, in the quarter-finals, they were to face Man City.

Since their heavy defeat in the league, things had changed. City may have been running away with the title, but this was now a different Liverpool side.

As expected, Coutinho had departed for Barcelona in January, for an astonishing 105 million. But that had given Jürgen the opportunity to add another piece to his Liverpool puzzle. He'd spent a mammoth 75 million on Southampton's Dutch centre-back, Virgil van Dijk.

It had felt like a lot at the time, but it had only taken one game for Virgil to start repaying his transfer fee, with the winning goal in a derby game against Everton.

That had been three months ago. Now, Liverpool had the small matter of the Champions League quarter-finals – against the team on the verge of clinching the Premier League title.

It also pitted Jürgen against his old rival, Pep Guardiola, the man who'd beaten him consistently during their time in Germany.

"We want to smother City," Jürgen said, encouraging his players before the game. "Never let them get their passes going, because once they do, they'll beat us."

Even in the dressing room, the players could hear the roaring of the Anfield crowd.

"Use the crowd tonight, guys," Jürgen continued. "Nobody else has an advantage like this. Nobody else can use this. The Kop are better than any new signing – it's like starting with a 1-0 lead."

"Remember when we played them in the league and

they beat us 5-0," Henderson added. "Sadio was sent off. This is our chance for justice."

"We win this, and we knock out the best team in the competition," Pep Lijnders chipped in. "We put ourselves in the driving seat."

The atmosphere in the stadium dwarfed anything Jürgen had ever experienced before, including his Dortmund days.

He strolled out of the tunnel and over towards Pep.

"Jürgen." Pep smiled warmly. He reached out and grabbed the Liverpool manager's hand. Jürgen pulled him in and slapped a hand across his back.

"Good to see you again," Jürgen grinned. "Just like Germany, huh?"

"Not quite," Pep said, shaking his head. "It never got this loud out there."

"No, not quite," Jürgen agreed.

On another day, they might have exchanged a few more words. In another world, they might have been good friends. But for the time being, they were rivals.

Liverpool came out quickly, swarming all over the City players and not giving them a moment to breathe.

It didn't take long for the first goal to come, and there were no surprises about the scorer. Mo Salah.

A moment later, it was two, when Oxlade-Chamberlain slammed in from 20 yards. And then it was three, when Sadio Mané rose in the air to head the ball home.

Liverpool had blitzed Man City. They'd played football the way Jürgen had always dreamed of it being played. This was pure football – high energy, chaotic and exciting. This was everything that he'd wanted since his very first days at Mainz.

In the second half, they demonstrated the other side of their skillset. This was the side that Jürgen wasn't so keen on, but the side that he knew was just as important. Liverpool were disciplined and responsible, slowing the pace down. City were powerless to fight back, because Jürgen's players controlled the game.

They saw out the 3-0 win. The second half hadn't been pretty, but it had been effective, and it was what was needed to win trophies.

And that was exactly what Jürgen intended to do.

18
SWEEPER KEEPER

December 2018, Anfield, Liverpool, England
Premier League, Liverpool v Everton

Two Champions League finals – two defeats.

That was the record that Jürgen had to his name. After crushing City, Liverpool had breezed past Roma in the semi-finals, to set up a mouth-watering final against twelve-times winners Real Madrid.

Despite losing Mo Salah to injury, they'd come back from 1-0 down in the second half. But then a couple of costly mistakes from Loris Karius in goal – and a ridiculous overhead kick from Gareth Bale – had won the game for Madrid.

But Liverpool had now shown that they could mix it with the best of them. City had won the league with a record 100 points, but Jürgen's side had beaten them three times. They could compete. They were ready.

Once more, Jürgen had to be shrewd in the transfer market. The arrivals of Mo Salah and Virgil van Dijk had shown that, with the right signings, even a single player could completely transform the team.

As ever, departures created opportunities for improvements.

Emre Can had left for Juventus, after refusing to sign a new contract. His absence had left a hole in the middle of Liverpool's midfield, and Jürgen filled it with two fresh players – Naby Keïta from RB Leipzig and Fabinho from AS Monaco.

"Fabinho is going to be so important to us," Jürgen told his coaches. "He's everything we need – tall, strong, a brilliant passer and tackler. He could fill in at centre-back – he's our version of Busquets."

His team had now mostly come together. The marauding full-backs, the dominant leader in the heart of defence, the box-to-box engine room midfielder, the tall and clever passer, and then the hard-working, electric front three.

There was just one piece missing.

At Borussia Dortmund, Roman Weidenfeller in goal had always been quick off his line, almost filling in as an extra outfield player. It was a role that was now popular with all the big clubs – none more so than in Manuel Neuer at Bayern Munich. The Sweeper Keeper.

At Liverpool, Jürgen had tried it with both Simon Mignolet and Loris Karius, without success. But his eye had been caught by a keeper that his Liverpool team had actually put five goals past at Anfield – the Roma and Brazil goalkeeper, Alisson.

"Look at where he starts," Jürgen told his scouts, as they studied a clip of Alisson. "He's ready to go before the ball is even in their half."

"And watch a couple of these passes," one of the scouts said, selecting another video.

Jürgen leaned forward, watching highlights of

Alisson spraying big, 60-yard passes to the streaking Roma attackers.

"That's a whole other dimension for us. Imagine Mo or Sadio going after those," Jürgen nodded.

Jürgen smiled. The departure of Coutinho had seemed like a disaster at the time but, without that, they wouldn't have been able to afford either van Dijk or Alisson. This was going to transform the team.

Now there was nobody left on Jürgen's shopping list. At last, he was confident – he had the perfect team.

It didn't take long to see what an addition Alisson was in goal. If a team pressed Liverpool closely, forcing them back, he could lift a brilliant ball forward to their attackers and ease the pressure on the defence.

Liverpool started the Premier League season with six straight wins. By the start of December, they were still unbeaten and had only drawn three matches. Yet, somehow, they were still behind Manchester City.

The next game was a huge one for anybody from the city of Liverpool. It was the Merseyside derby, Liverpool v Everton.

"We need this to keep pace with City," Jürgen told

his boys. "We're going for the title. They know it. We know it. And Everton know it too."

"They will fight for everything today, boys," Pep Lijnders continued. "Forget about form. They will fight to the very end. They don't want us to win the title."

"I know a lot of you aren't from around here," Jürgen added, "but this game means everything to the fans out there. Show them that you care."

Despite the distance between the two teams in the league table, the game was tight. Everton had chances – which were quickly blocked by Alisson in goal.

With time ticking away, Jürgen turned to his bench. He'd been in title races with Dortmund, and he'd won and lost titles. He knew that, at this stage in the league, every point was crucial. Liverpool couldn't afford to slip too far behind Man City.

On came Daniel Sturridge and Divock Origi. Given the form of Liverpool's front three, both had struggled for game time.

"This is an opportunity to prove yourself," Jürgen told them. "Go and win a place in the first eleven."

With time ticking on, the ball was launched into the

Everton box. It was hit clear as far as van Dijk, who hooked it high, back into the area.

Pickford, the Everton keeper, struggled to get beneath the ball and, as he went to palm it out, he mistakenly hit it back into play – exactly to where Divock Origi was lurking. He met the ball with his head and flicked it into the back of the net.

Liverpool had won. In the final minute, they had secured three vital points.

Jürgen sprinted onto the pitch, punching the air and leaping off the ground. He was met by his new goalkeeper, Alisson, and they jumped into each other's arms.

This was huge. It felt like one of the greatest moments of his career.

This was what his Liverpool team were all about. They would never give up.

19

A BIGGER TROPHY SHELF

December 2019, Khalifa International Stadium, Doha, Qatar
Club World Cup Final, Liverpool v Flamengo

It had been an incredible year.

Jürgen had ended his own personal trophy drought in epic style, winning the Champions League, against Tottenham Hotspur.

Liverpool had lost just one game in the whole of the Premier League season. Yet, as it turned out, that hadn't been enough. Liverpool had pushed the eventual champions, Man City, all the way, but ultimately they'd fallen short on the final day.

Despite this disappointment, Liverpool had set their own club record with their total points for the season, and they'd achieved a Champions League win. They'd then continued their success in the following season, winning the European Super Cup, beating Chelsea on penalties.

Jürgen had exactly the squad he wanted, so there'd been very few transfers in the summer, with only a couple of players going in and out.

He'd been clear with his players during the pre-season.

"It's going to be the Premier League title, guys," he'd told them. "Thirty years ago – that was the last time this city saw a league title. It's on us to bring it back. We have the team. I believe we can do it."

They began the season with eight consecutive wins and then, after a draw with Manchester United, they continued winning games. With 3-1 wins over City and Arsenal, and a 2-1 win at Chelsea, it was clear that Liverpool were becoming unstoppable.

If Salah wasn't scoring, Mané or Firmino would step up.

Off the bench, Origi was in brilliant form as a super-sub, and Wijnaldum, Henderson and Fabinho had formed a brilliant midfield three. There were no weak links in the team.

By the middle of December, Liverpool were ten points clear and still unbeaten.

But now there was the small matter of the Club World Cup in Qatar. This was where Liverpool could cement themselves as the best team in the world.

They'd already battled past Monterrey in the semi-finals, to set up a final against Flamengo, the champions from South America.

There had been some who'd wanted Jürgen to make changes for this game. There was a busy league schedule coming up, and the Club World Cup didn't have as much prestige. Jürgen's own assistant, Pep Lijnders, wanted to see changes for the game too.

"It doesn't matter," he argued. "You said it yourself, Jürgen. It's the league title we want."

"But this game makes us world champions," Jürgen insisted. "We get to go back home as champions of the world. It will be good for the guys to get their hands on another trophy. They earned this by winning the Champions League."

He was able to name his strongest starting line-up for the final. Most fans and pundits expected them to thrash Flamengo, but Jürgen knew better than to assume it would be easy. The Brazilian club were supported by all their fans, urging their players on to win the final and come back as heroes.

It took until extra time for Liverpool to make their breakthrough. A swift counter-attack fell to Mané, who fed the ball to Roberto Firmino. The Brazilian striker rounded the keeper and drilled the ball into the net.

Liverpool had held on. They'd won their second trophy of the season and become the world champions.

"It's weird isn't it?" Jürgen remarked after the game. "We're champions of the world, but it doesn't feel like the biggest achievement."

"Champions of the world, but not champions of England," Lijnders laughed.

"Yet," Jürgen added.

20
MORE THAN CHAMPIONS

July 2020, Anfield, Liverpool, England
Premier League, Liverpool v Aston Villa

"It should feel different, shouldn't it?" Jordan Henderson said, as they entered the home dressing room at Anfield.

There was an eerie silence in the room. It wasn't long before kick-off, and normally the stadium would be alive with noise. Even down in the dressing rooms, they would have been able to hear the chanting of the fans.

But today, all they could hear was their own chatter.

It had been like this since the middle of March. Liverpool had been only a few games away from sealing their first Premier League title – their first league title in 30 years – when the season had been brought to a dramatic halt.

The coronavirus pandemic had swept around the world. People hadn't been allowed in close contact with each other – and football had been no exception. It hadn't been until June that the football season had restarted, and even then it had returned without fans.

In recent years, Liverpool had turned Anfield into something of a fortress, and that had been helped massively by the presence of their vocal fan base. Jürgen hadn't been sure how much his team would be affected by the absence of that support.

They had begun with a 0-0 draw away at Everton, before a 4-0 win over Crystal Palace had put them within reach of the title.

They'd known then that, if Man City lost to Chelsea, Liverpool would be champions.

Under normal circumstances, the players would have gathered round and watched the game together. But

COVID had meant that this was impossible. Instead, the players watched the game at home, flooding the group chat with messages.

"PULISIC! City have lost this."

"City level. Let's focus on the next one, boys."

"PENALTY."

"WILLIAN!"

"JUST HOLD ON."

"We've done it."

Jürgen hadn't got involved in the group chat – he'd barely been able to watch the game. But Liverpool *had* done it. Without needing to step out on the pitch, Liverpool had been confirmed as Premier League champions.

The next game had been away at Man City and, in the aftermath of their celebrations, Liverpool had been beaten 4-0. It was a loss, but they'd won the big prize.

The team was then back at Anfield and, despite the absence of fans, Jürgen wanted his players to keep their focus.

"It won't feel different until the fans are back," Milner told Henderson.

"Let's focus, boys!" Jürgen beckoned to his players. "Last time wasn't good enough. I know we're champions. I know we've worked hard to get here and we just want to relax. But there's six games left until the season ends."

"There's records at stake," Henderson added.

"Right," Jürgen said. "We can be more than *just* champions. We can be the greatest team in Premier League history. We can enter those record books. The fans aren't here today, but they made Anfield our fortress. They carried us through games we wouldn't have won otherwise. And they're all at home, watching us. Win this game for them. Show the world we deserve to be champions."

Aston Villa were the next opponents. They gave Liverpool a guard of honour before the game, then battled hard. It took two late goals, including one from youngster Curtis Jones, for Liverpool to seal a 2-0 win.

Jürgen smiled as his team came off the pitch. They'd done what many had believed to be impossible when he'd taken over at the club.

And they'd done it his way.

21
UNLIKELY HERO

May 2021, Hawthorns, West Bromwich, England
Premier League, Liverpool v West Bromwich Albion

"That title win seems a world away now," Jürgen sighed, as he slumped in his seat, next to Pep Lijnders.

"We're still the champions," Lijnders reminded him.

"No, we're not," Jürgen corrected him. "City have already won it."

Jürgen still wasn't sure where it had all gone so wrong. The summer had been a success. They'd snapped up two big signings, in Thiago Alcântara and Diogo Jota, and they'd kept all their big names. They'd even started the season with three consecutive wins.

But it had all started to come unstuck away at Aston Villa. Liverpool had put out a full-strength team and they'd been battered 7-2. Then the injuries had begun.

Thiago, van Dijk, Alisson, Joe Gomez and Matip had all found themselves injured at one stage or another. Liverpool had then been forced to field youngsters Nat Phillips and Rhys Williams at centre-back. On occasion, Jürgen even had to move Fabinho back to cover.

In February and March, they'd lost six of their seven games. This included a run of six consecutive defeats at Anfield. The stadium that had once been their fortress suddenly became a place where they were completely vulnerable.

Teams that hadn't won at Anfield for years were turning up and picking up wins.

Worse even than that, Liverpool hadn't scored in any of the games. It hadn't just been the defence that wasn't doing its job – they'd become toothless in attack. Firmino had been way off the pace and Mané had been quiet.

The title was gone, they were out of the cups, and now they were in a battle simply to get into the top four. They just needed to qualify for the Champions League.

This meant that their next match, away at West Brom, was huge. There were three games left – and Liverpool sat in fifth. The two teams above them, Leicester and Chelsea, were still to play each other. If Liverpool won all their games, they would qualify for the Champions League. But they *had* to win every game.

"We know what we need to do today, guys," Jürgen said. "It's simple. There are no away goals to worry about. We just need to win."

"Whatever it takes," Fabinho added, "make it count."

As was common this season, Liverpool started poorly and quickly fell a goal behind. But gradually, they began to find their rhythm.

Fabinho and Thiago began to play their passes, and it didn't take long for Salah to get Liverpool level.

Then the onslaught began.

West Brom held firm, with black and white shirts flying in front of every Liverpool shot.

"Forward! Forward!" Jürgen urged his players.

This was no time for tactics – just intense, attacking football, with Liverpool pushing their attacking players forward.

But time was ticking on, with the scores still level. 70th minute. 80th minute. 90th minute … Liverpool needed inspiration from somewhere.

With just a minute to go, Liverpool won a corner.

"Everyone up! Come on!" Jürgen bellowed.

He ushered everyone forward, including his keeper, Alisson, who glanced at him questioningly.

One last chance.

The ball from Trent was perfect. It was whipped in, curling through the air. Jürgen found himself leaping up – as if he could get his own head on it.

Instead, it was his goalkeeper, Alisson, who met the ball. He rose high, meeting it with a powerful header that he flicked towards the far corner. It flew past the West Brom keeper, landing in the back of the net.

Liverpool had won the game.

"This team never gives in," Jürgen told Lijnders. "Never. We are getting back in the Champions League. We are coming back."

22
JÜRGEN'S WAY

May 2022, Wembley Stadium, London, England
FA Cup Final, Liverpool v Chelsea

"There'll come a year when Man City won't be as good," Jürgen moaned.

This season, Liverpool had once more been involved in a title race with their main rivals. They had also snatched a place in the Champions League, thanks to Alisson's late goal against West Brom near the end of last season.

And with their players now starting to return from injury, Liverpool were making progress.

"You know we're going to be playing every possible game this season," Lijnders remarked to Jürgen.

"Don't remind me," Jürgen groaned. "I'm exhausted just thinking about it."

Only a few months earlier, they'd won their first trophy of the season, with a penalty shootout victory over Chelsea in the final of the League Cup.

They'd also battled their way through the Champions League, eliminating Benfica and Inter Milan on their way. Now, in just two weeks' time, they had the final – against Real Madrid, a rematch from four years ago.

Liverpool were on the brink of an unprecedented quadruple – the League Cup, the FA Cup, the Champions League *and* the Premier League title.

They could become legends.

In the FA Cup final, they were taking on Chelsea – the same opponents that they'd met in the League Cup final. There were also two Premier League games taking place in the following week, and the small matter of the Champions League final in a fortnight.

But today, the focus was Chelsea, in the FA Cup.

Jürgen had a full-strength team to choose from. He'd opted for a new centre-back, Ibrahima Konaté, behind the midfield trio of Keïta, Henderson and Thiago. The plan was to smother a Chelsea team that would use five at the back.

Further forward, Sadio Mané was playing as striker, supported by Mo Salah and Luis Díaz.

"We beat these guys in February," Jürgen reminded his players. "It went all the way to penalties then. I don't want that today. I want this job done in 90 minutes. We know how Chelsea play. They want Jorginho on the ball. If we stop him, we stop them."

Luis Díaz was the new man for Liverpool, having joined the club in January. He'd been explosive since his arrival, forcing his way into the starting line-up. His form meant that Sadio Mané had been moved inside to accommodate him.

"Run at them, Luis," Jürgen told his new signing. "No instructions, just run. Reece James will push on. You'll have the space."

It didn't take long for disaster to strike. Half an hour

in, Mo Salah was hauled off injured, and was replaced by Diogo Jota.

"Another final where we've lost Mo," Jürgen grumbled.

But this time, Liverpool had the quality in depth to carry on. Jota was far better than any player they'd had on the bench previously, and they continued to dominate.

The game was played at a high intensity. Luis Díaz was central to Liverpool's play, cutting inside and firing a series of shots at the Chelsea goal.

This was football played the Jürgen Klopp way. It was the football that had got him to four Champions League finals – the football that had won Liverpool their first Premier League title.

Every tackle was met with a huge roar, and every time Liverpool came forward, the fans rose in their seats.

With the pandemic rules now relaxed, it was great to have the fans back in the stadium, and no doubt the Liverpool fans had a huge impact on Liverpool's form. But Chelsea held firm. They were managed by Thomas Tuchel, a man who'd taken on the Dortmund and

Mainz jobs after Jürgen. He'd also won the Champions League only the previous year.

Extra time rolled around and Liverpool came back out without van Dijk, who'd picked up an injury. By now, both teams had given their all. They were exhausted.

At the end of extra time, there were still no goals. Both teams knew what that meant.

Penalties.

"Penalties are a lottery," Jürgen told his players. "Pick your spot early. Hit it hard. We've got this."

On only the second penalty, Chelsea's César Azpilicueta struck the post. Now Liverpool had the advantage.

"Come on," Jürgen growled, gritting his teeth.

Every other penalty was scored, until it came to Sadio Mané. He had the opportunity to win it for Liverpool. But his spotkick was poor, and it was palmed away by his compatriot, Édouard Mendy, in goal.

Then, a moment later, Liverpool had the advantage once again, when Alisson saved from Mount.

Kostas Tsimikas was up next. If he scored, Liverpool would win it.

Once more, it was out of Jürgen's hands. He could only watch and pray from the side-lines.

"Come on, Kostas," he muttered under his breath. He didn't want to shout any instructions – he couldn't risk putting Kostas off.

The shot was struck well, and Jürgen could already see Mendy going the wrong way. If it was on target, it was a goal.

Tsimikas had beaten Mendy – *and* it was on target. Liverpool had won the FA Cup.

It wasn't the biggest trophy Jürgen had won in his time at Liverpool, but it felt significant. They were now just a few games away from a possible quadruple.

With their first FA Cup, Jürgen had now won every domestic trophy there was to win with Liverpool.

He thought back to his younger days and his struggles to find real success as a player. He'd never expected to make it as a player, and he'd never thought he would make it as a manager either.

But now, he was one of the best managers in the world. He was on the verge of history.

And he'd done it all his way. The Jürgen Klopp way.

HOW MANY
HAVE YOU READ?

MESSI KANE RONALDO HAALAND SALAH

PULISIC LEWANDOWSKI MAHREZ MBAPPÉ SON

   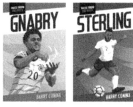

SAKA SANCHO FÉLIX GNABRY STERLING

RASHFORD KANTÉ SILVA VAN DIJK

SOUTHGATE GUARDIOLA KLOPP